How The

Light Changes

ALSO BY STEVE SPENCE

A Curious Shipwreck, Shearsman Books, 2010
Limits of Control, Penned in the Margins, 2011
Maelstrom Origami, Shearsman Books, 2014
Many Red Fish, Knives, Forks and Spoons Press, 2019
Eat Here, Get Gas & Worms, Red Ceilings Press, 2021

ANTHOLOGIES

In the Presence of Sharks, Phlebas, 2006
Orphans of Albion, Survivors Press/The Sixties Press, 2008
The Forward Book of Poetry, Forward Press, 2011
Smartarse, Knives, Forks and Spoons Press, 2011
Adventures in Form, Penned in the Margins, 2012
The Robin Hood Book, Caparison, 2012
The Brown Envelope Book, Culture Matters, 2021

How The Light Changes

Steve Spence

Shearsman Books

First published in the United Kingdom in 2021 by
Shearsman Books Ltd
PO Box 4239
Swindon
SN3 9FN

Shearsman Books Ltd Registered Office
30–31 St. James Place, Mangotsfield, Bristol BS16 9JB
(this address not for correspondence)

www.shearsman.com

ISBN 978-1-84861-790-2

ACKNOWLEDGMENTS
Some of these poems have been
previously published in the following:
The Rialto, *Shearsman* magazine,
Stride and *Tears in the Fence*.

CONTENTS

She Breathes Unsteadily

Everything
here seems
strangely
familiar.
Not every-
one thinks
that robot
terminators
are a good
idea but a
purge has
already begun
and our team
are now on
the home
stretch. First
we have to
find the right
location. "It's
just as likely
that many
things do eat
jellyfish", he
said. Yet this
is not a defence
of liberal
democracy
and it's that
extra flash
of colour that
makes all the
difference.
"It may be
a way of

staying alive
if you have
a terminal
disease", he
said.

A Coastline
Like No Other

When you look
at the pictures
now the word
that comes to
mind is hubris.
Yet their part-
nership began
in a curious
way and there's
nothing to
be gained by
seeking the
middle-ground.
Are we still
tilting at wind-
mills? Now, if
there's nothing
else, my sausage
sandwich is
congealing.
What you're
suggesting here
is that false
memories are
being implanted.
My, how the sky
has suddenly
darkened yet
undemanding
and distracting
is what we
need just now.
Isn't it about
time we joined

up the dots?
Then, in his
own words –
"the downhill
slope started".

Tear It Up

"Globalisation
is here to stay",
she said. When
it comes to coins
it's all about the
condition yet
drinks trolleys
are making a
comeback for
those who want
to serve in style.
"It's time to stalk
the margins again",
she said. You're
not in biochemistry,
are you?" "Yet his
background is as
intriguing and varied
as his recipes", she said.
As we draw near it's
clear the nocturnal
scavengers have
been out in force.
Did I hear a hurdy
gurdy in there some-
where? Despite its
apparent simplicity
Summertime has its
hidden depths. Yet
the fish are jumping
and the cotton is high.
How many of these
rooms are occupied?
Here we have sound
clusters which create

a mood of density
and thickness. Once
you're extinct there's
no coming back.
"It ain't necessarily
so", she said.

How The
Light Changes

This is like
food in an
art gallery,
it looks so
alluring.
If you're
here on a
windy day
it's a bit like
the Sahara
yet all these
molluscs are
filter feeders
and in any
case we don't
exactly run
a tight ship.
How I still
love Nina
Simone's
version of
*Here Comes
the Sun.*
"Shyness
turns you into
an onlooker",
she said. It's
an elegant
solution to
an insoluble
problem but
sometimes a
beautiful
beach is

simply too
hard to resist.
Once again
nature is
screaming
at us from
the sky.
"It's high
time I went
for another
swim", she
said.

Taking Aim
At Art

Our only option
is to use a net.
Have you got
a book about
fish and how
to look after
them? What
do we need
to make a
wave farm
work? Roger
Scruton is
going on about
Wagner again
while Nigella
is tending an egg.
"My speciality
is offshore energy",
she said. Once a
crab has shed its
skin it has to run
for cover yet
some new words
catch on while
others disappear.
Do you live and
sleep with both
eyes open? "Patti
Smith's blend of
poetry and music
is quite specific",
she said. Once again
we are in a state
of paralysis and

disarray. Green
crabs are quick
learners. "I always
enjoyed physics
and maths", she said.

A
Navigational
Error

Stagnation
remains a
profound
worry yet
we did all
we could
to mask
these sounds.
We can't
always
believe
what we
hear yet
for bees,
colour is
a matter
of life
and death.
Have the
heady
perfumes
permeated
the onions
yet? There
are no
contracts
and no career
plans. Do you
enjoy the films
of Peter
Greenaway?
At this

point in
the
proceedings
it's
usually
best to
flake the
salmon.

Trapped In
The Wreckage

"There's a
good chance
that you're
close to a
whistling
beach",
she said.
It's an orange
swirl, if
you will.
Are you
still trying
to face in
both directions
at the same
time? Yet a
bizarre
torrent of
water rushes
across the
landscape
and this year
may be the
warmest on
record. "These
islands have a
life of their
own", he said.
Do you have
any faith in the
current peace
process? "I'm
guided by the
beauty of our

weapons",
sang Leonard.

Running
For Cover

Deference to
authority is
a much wider
problem but
it's alarming
how much
plastic there
is in the sea.
Once again
we've been
caught in the
crossfire.
What part
does culture
play in kindness?
Is it a dab or
is it a crab?
"This is a
perfect speed
of drift", he said.
Extreme tides
mean that ocean
predators may
find their way
some distance
inland. We may
now see increasing
numbers of police
on the streets.
Yes, but you can
never use the
word 'surely'
when you're
talking about

infinity. How
then can we
draw a tree
differently?
"I felt at home
in the crowds,
amid the hum
and the neon",
he said.

Leaning Into
The Wind

Some claim
that to look
in to the eye
of a whale
is a life-
changing
experience.
Every element
of the scene
is independently
familiar.
Is a turd the
ultimate
ready-made?
"People have
to listen to
the arguments",
she said.
Who needs
magic when
intricate
engineering
can give life
to the inanimate?
These blacktip
sharks have
adapted to swim
in less than a
foot of water.
Hence their woolly
coats. "We'll be
holding his feet
to the fire on
this issue", he said.

What's with the
wig? When it comes
to what we see
the brain often
overrides the
eyes.

A Ripening Fruit

What do we think
about the gig economy?
In astronomical terms
comets are tiny. Have
you ever seen a cat on
a lead? "It's a cross
between a trout and
a pollack", she said.
Clive Lewis is a class
act and needs to be
encouraged. "Art
without ideas is simply
decoration, isn't it?",
she said. From where
we're sitting we need
something to bargain
with but there remains
a broad tension between
capital and labour,
whatever the pundits
are saying. "We eat with
our eyes", she said,
"but our ears are just
as important". Foxes,
of course, are just about
everywhere yet words
relating to property
theft dominate, while
self-hooking rigs are
now the norm. "Barbed
wire is a weapon of
mass-destruction", he
said. Do you paint
pictures with your feet?
Yet good data, even in

large volumes, does not
ensure you will arrive
at the truth. "You don't
want a fox in your head",
she said.

A Note
Of Anxiety

Sometimes
collecting
can be as
creative a
process as
making.
Do you
keep a
weather
diary?
"I hate it
when she
uses my
arguments
against me",
she said.
Is it just
the leaves
that quiver?
There are
only two
ways to
go with
squid –
low and
slow or
quickly
at a high
heat. Are
we in or
out of the
single market?
Yes, but
do you

hesitate
when you
think?

Slicing The Surface

Why are
Italy's
banks in
crisis?
Yet the
darkness
tells us
a great
deal about
ourselves.
Who exactly
is this third
man? "The
past is the
accumulated
life of any-
one", he said.
Is conceptual
art always
emotionally
dry? Where
are the red
drapes? "I
love the
insouciant
air of the
wolf", she
said. When
it comes to
conceptual
art it's the
thought that
counts. There's
something

understated
about these
images and
it's always
worth
encouraging
your mind
to wander.

The Endless Blue

At this point in the game a smooth transition
of power is not on the agenda. "It may be a
question of self-defence rather than colonial

oppression", he said. Are you questioning my
methods? "Beauty is so often uncounted as a
factor in his work", she said. Here the cold waves

clatter like wrecked fuselage. Is the world economy
being kept alive by money printing? Flavour may
include sound as well as taste, smell and colour

but this re-branding exercise is hopefully
doomed to failure. Once again it's a question
of managing our expectations. "It was more

a matter of the skyline playing me than me
playing the skyline", he said. Yet there are
trigger points here which work horizontally

as well as vertically and we need to put a firewall
in place. "This time we're after big perch", he said.
It's a good way of utilising a difficult space yet

there's a constant shift of audience here and it
may prove impossible to separate one sense from
another. Are you worried that we're moving too

slowly? *This Was* is an underrated album and
Mick Abrahams is a great blues guitarist yet
celebrity culture has surely gone beyond the pale.

Expanding The Search Area

"Each to their own", she said. We will have
to try an entirely new approach yet surface
water flooding is also expected and it's what

happens after you hook one that makes the
difference. "It's a very selfish lifestyle", he
said, after having admitted that he got his

first shotgun at the age of sixteen. If it's not
neo-liberal it's not going to happen. Has anyone
sued yet? "Once upon a time I was a game-

keeper but now I'm a poacher", he said. These
drawings aren't made by pushing a rake across
a surface yet alongside walking and storytelling

it's a very human thing to do. Here we have the
basic principles of fingerprint analysis. Now the
biting makes sense. Is there such a thing as

incontrovertible evidence? "Yet the more we look
at the cosmos the stranger it becomes", she said.
Do you ever suffer from indecision? You don't

know what's around the corner if you bite into
something that's unsafe yet nature is full of design
flaws that we're all trying to fix. Next time you

fancy doing something really frustrating, try
balancing a pencil on its sharpened tip. "Set
me free from what exactly?", she said.

An Expert In The Field

"Perfection belongs only to narrated
events", she said. When are we planning
on going to the lake? Let's venture into

the maze. Are you a creative powerhouse?
Sometimes an exit turns out to be a new
opening but trusting your gut instinct is

not a reliable way to size people up. Today
we're using a float for bite indication. Dozens
of fish disappear in a flash yet the intelligence

may be more in the data than in the algorithm.
Even more baffling are the three large holes
blown into the ground yet our swirling shoal

has nowhere to go and feeding begins. "Some
still view the multiverse as an abdication of
scientific responsibility", she said. Can we

choose which memories to keep and which
to get rid of? For instance, some bacteria kill
themselves as soon as they are infected by a

virus. Here we have a series of layered compos-
itions. What do you think about the knife angel?
Growing up destined to live in water means there

are many skills to master yet in the darkness
the crabs can feel their surroundings. Why is
it useful to be able to recognise voices at all?

An Underwater Shot

It's all to do with the tidal cycle. "We have
a clear view of what society could be like but
we have no way of getting there", he said.

Suddenly, there's this awkward, swirling
wind. "A coherent script is a good starting
point", she said. Navigating by the stars is

never an easy thing to do but for now this
remains a capricious co-existence. When
you're creating an engraving you have to

press really hard to allow the paper to soak
up the ink. "I'd still like to get a thousand
out of it", he said. What happens next depends

on what you think money actually is. Are we
in the presence of a domestic drama? "Surely
our current form of globalisation has a design

fault yet an information economy may not be
compatible with a market economy", he said.
Are we capable of striking populist gestures?

"Mr Steed, how resplendent you look", she
said. In a way they have grasped that if climate
change is real, capitalism is finished. Yet an

hour of physical activity a day is the ideal and
our next tactic is to target the margin. How literal
can we be about the skyline as a starting point?

A State Of Unease

Are you having intrusive thoughts?
In fact, the shortening days stir
them into action and here we have

a description of the wind, not an
explanation of its behaviour. Yet
we need to register even the tiniest

of bites and once again the sharks
are here. "It was always a question
of tightly controlled storyboarding

plus the music of Bernard Hermann",
he said. Is this another form of empire
building? Traditionally, mind wandering

has been seen in a negative light,
though to be fair we literally have
all the time in the world and our

baiting pattern has yet to get going.
Ring ring ring ring ring – "Hello, can
I speak to Mr Steve Spence please?".

On your bike, laddie, I'm busy and
these calls are becoming intrusive.
When the storm hit we couldn't stay

at home and other scenarios suggested
themselves. Once again his dreams
were all about returning to the sea.

Another Vital Clue

"There's a random element at work
here", she said. What do you do at
the seaside when it's raining? "It's

a question of varying the tackle and
changing your bait", he said. We could
always look at new ways of helping

people report what they eat of course
though you might want to search the
premises while you're here. "In this

music there are lots of conversations
happening between the past and the
present", she said. If they decide to

attack you are unlikely to see it coming
as our economy is a world of complex,
chance events, not simple wave forms.

Eventually, we were shown into a small
rear bedroom. Shall we not cherish the
juxtaposition? When the water's racing

through you get a lot of tiny knocks on
the rod tip but we don't recognise poly-
gamy and our tattoos are never just skin-

deep. If you're on a low income what's
the point of saving? "As soon as I got on
my horse everything changed", he said.

A Mistaken Identity

"Long before I became a psychologist
I was interested in people", he said.
This event is due to more than stormy

weather and the mind also plays a vital
role in creating such nebulous shapes.
Have you ever seen anybody walk on

clouds? Yet it's a perfect day for the
dragonfly and what I saw last summer
is nothing compared to what is coming.

What does it mean to do nothing? In the
ground floor hallway hangs a massive
monochrome collage. "Wherever I go I

ask questions about economics and get
answers about climate", he said. This is
more than just a research exercise and

outside my window the birds are gathering
in numbers. The patterns they are creating
in the sky are astonishing. What brings these

figures together? Storms may also create
artwork in the sky yet there remains a point-
less argument between economists and ecol-

ogists over which crisis is more important.
People say they feel they're a part of the city
when their communities are included on the map.

Contorting The Clouds

"It's a virus that's spreading", he said.
Truth has become a matter of opinion
but gravity is still gravity and it's a

symptom of a failing education system.
Yet the dragonfly is a beautiful beast
and infinity remains an extraordinary

and puzzling concept. For these reasons,
followers of the cognitive view argue
that grammar alone is not enough to

understand language. Would you carry
out surgery on yourself in order to survive?
"Yet there is ambiguity and there is a

filtering out of sound from the landscape",
he said. Nevertheless, our problem is largely
a technical one and when you consider the

physics of a wave form it becomes even
more beautiful. How do we translate the
landscape into sound? "I'm more interested

in the quality of the narrative", he said. Are
you a beautiful troublemaker? Yet subtly, the
sense of what it means to be a 'worker' has

changed. What emerges from this shattered dream
and when did you last think about Basil Brush?
As the tension escalates the weather worsens.

Hollowed Out

There are limits to what the state can do
but it retains some real power. Is everybody
happy? "You bet your life we are", she said.

Which clinics at the moment are the best
placed to offer these technologies? "We're
very close to another weather front", he said.

What happens in *Hamlet*? Much of this stems
from a loss of a sense of historical mission
yet it's a shoal fish, the bream, and it's Ophelia

who saves the day. Is it any wonder that there
is a clamour for longing? If you're in the breeze
it can still feel quite chilly as huge imbalances

of power are being created in networked
societies. Nobody talks about 'the left' any
more but one day you'll meet the devil in

the wood and lager isn't quite the same as
absinthe, in any case. Today, more than ever,
science is expensive but we need to encourage

curiosity and free-thinking is still on the agenda.
"It may be that this bird is interpreting what it
hears rather than simply replicating the sounds",

she said. Are we making more spelling mistakes
than ever? "If there's a beast in man it has its
match in woman", she said. Where is the evidence?

A Pawn Shop

Is our resolve being tested again? Our buzzard
has disappeared but the two crows still appear to
be harrying each other. Do space and time really

exist and can we understand the deep textures
of the universe? "These are blood drops produced
by the impact of the weapon", she said. Have you

come to shake a leg? Yet he was a bond trader
by day and a pharmaceutical spy by night – in
which case exactly the opposite has happened and

this is a truly unspoilt habitat, packed with wildlife.
"I was like a kid in a candy shop again", she said.
As the seas keep warming the kelp forests are

retreating further south but alternative theories
suggest that the purpose of sleep is to conserve
energy. "You think I'm just a tatty old music hall

actor, don't you", he said. Sleep is the price we
pay for learning. Yes but why would you spend
several hours a day at the mercy of a predator?

It's simply a matter of living in the moment yet
there may need to be a period of readjustment and
breaking even will be a lot better than losing money.

What about some shelving around the wall? "It's as
if my mind creates shapes I don't know about", she said.
In the dim light the grey salt dunes run on for miles.

A Conflict Resolution

When we arrived at the insect house there
were no insects. Yet all over the world the
establishment is desperately circling the

wagons and in pushing my way through
some of the guy ropes came unstuck. "Mind
you, dragonflies don't usually hang around",

he said. When did you last see a greater-
crested grebe? "You can't have a no-fly-zone
that excludes one of the key protagonists but

many people think this is an exaggerated story
and the main thing we are up against is super-
stition", he said. To a certain extent writing is

always about lone gratification yet we may need
some historical context here. Do you think the
coup was organised by hardcore secularists?

Once again the trend is towards a one-party
authoritarian state. "Each picture contains a mixture
of writing, painting and crayon scribbles while

this section consists of a series of small and
murky images", he said. What is it specifically
about words that appeals to you as a medium?

"All palaces are temporary places", he said, "but
I can't be an antidote to capitalism on my own".
"It's not an oak tree, it's a glass of water", she said.

A Panel Of Experts

If you haul these fish to the surface they
are likely to explode. "All I ever wanted
to do was be the singer in *The Who*", said

Roger. Yet filter feeders are on the march
and this is a perfect starter home for a
hermit crab. "We think you're more suited

to a strategic role", he said, but at his time
of life a strategic role wasn't on anyone's
agenda. What kind of creature is likely to

benefit from such a sheltered environment?
Are you a rewriter or a debunker of history?
Next we're heading inland and out onto the

frozen lake. "It's all about turning anxiety into
art", he said "and I quite enjoy quoting from
other sources". Even non-thinking life-forms

seem to have some inkling of this and in any
case nothing happens entirely by accident. If
this data turns out to be incorrect we are not

serving the public interest yet they say that
every skyline tells a story. "It's about time
I started to wear bright colours again", she said.

Here we have a strange and wonderful array
of found objects. "Here we have the jigging rod
and here we have the jigging lure", he said.

Surveying A Habitat

Are you still looking for signs and
meanings in the skies? "This is what
happens when somebody has a fish

and somebody else wants it", she said.
Is the universe as flat as a pancake?
Unless somebody has some amazing

flash of insight I think we are going to
carry on not having a clue. Today the
winds will be moderate and fresh but this

is a town humming with modernity as a
host of talented amateurs join in. "Yes, but
our robots aren't here just to make you look

cool", she said. We each organise what
we perceive and create our own version
of it yet water habitats vary dramatically

across the globe while working with colour
is like playing the piano. "Is it the ghost of
Liberace", he asked. Humans learn how to

do lots of things by watching someone else
but programming a new skill into a robot is
more difficult. Are these charts astronomical?

May I ask a philosophical question about
the nature of capitalism? When the robot is
stationary its feelings of embodiment are low.

A Shrinking Territory

"This conflict is not going to be resolved
by military action alone", he said. Yet the
river is still not safe to swim in and there is

little belief in the current peace mechanism.
"We may use an old harmonium to create the
sound of the traffic", he said, but we are in

a last resort situation and there are still six
weeks of the current administration to run.
Here we have long hours of boredom followed

by moments of high excitement. "It's a
shattering Chicago frenetic blues", she said
"and overall it's a rollicking raucous record".

On this occasion the rioters are from a new
constituency while the predators have large
eyes and extremely good vision. "It's beyond

satire this time", he said, "although a recount
has been initiated". More outside interference
is the last thing we need at this point in time.

"There's a roughness to his voice and it's
more 'full circle' than 'cultural appropriation'",
she said. Meanwhile, at home, we have more

weasel words from more weasel politicians.
It wasn't very slack when you picked the rod up
was it? "Irresistible explosive sounds", she said.

An Urban Disorder

Today is everything it is because
of yesterday but here we have a
new form of data-saving network

and it's best to have a culture of
open discussion. A skeletal musician
is hunched over his guitar. "Here

we have a sleazy bar-room singer
and here we have the theatre of
dreams", he said. Have we got colour

yet? "I was an assembler in a factory
producing pine furniture", he said.
It's a question of creating your own

picture or narrative from the abstraction
but when it comes to organising change
the network can function better than a

hierarchy. "There's some red there but
you can't quite discern it" he said. Are
you always so obsessive? Some bloke

has just won the ignoble prize for living
like a goat for three days yet our universe
has been around for nearly fourteen billion

years and it could all vanish in the blink
of an eye. Did you know that a good
troller is constantly readjusting his tackle?

A Question Of Telepathy

"What matters is not the amount of light but
the energy of each grain", he said. Are you
an ambitious man, Mr Neff? What you need

more than anything right now is a friend.
Have you ever seen a fiddler crab? Yet
electrons are often nowhere and this is

the famous quantum leap. Where are the
sinister clowns? Here we are talking about
the false memory of the individual rather

than the false memory of the film. Due to
such indeterminacy things are constantly
open to random change. Why do crabs move

sideways? "It's never a matter of things but
a matter of process", he said. Are we talking
about UFOs' here or are we talking about

scary clowns? Yes, but what has tarpaulin
got to do with a history of transgression?
"I loathe Trump", she said, "but I think he's

a very frightened man just now". After all,
how we sound is an essential part of who we
are and it depends on what you mean by justice.

"Reality is reduced to interaction", she said.
Ian MacMillan is reading the news. "We may
be on the brink of what we don't know", he said.

Looking At The Options

"We need the right trees in the right places",
he said. Here we have the surface popper yet
local knowledge remains the key and a detailed

map will help with access. A robot has started
learning to cook by watching a video of people
in a kitchen. Peter Vaughan has died. "The world

of art is not my speciality", he said, "though it's
one of my favourite eye-shadow colours and there's
a rumour about a dress". Are we slipping into

deforestation? We've only been here about ten
minutes and we've caught a fish already. Yet the
parrot crossbill has the biggest bill of all and it's

all lure fishing from now on. "We need the right
trees in all the right places", she said. A good teacher
will understand that a robot has a different way of

perceiving the world but this one is dressed like
a fabulously turned-out carrion crow with feathers
on her head. Here we have a rigid adherence to a

system of light and dark. Are you a modern architect,
Mr Kracklite? Yet a painting is a visual work of art
that demands to be seen on its own visual terms. Why

do we think prisons are so important? "Always keep
in mind that big bass work extremely close to shore",
he said. The implications of this are enormous.

Filling In The Dots

These bright colours look like they've
been painted into the clouds. "Not every-
one agrees with our methods", he said.

Yes, but can we seriously remove ourselves
from the picture? To the rock fisherman, this
place is a paradise. "So much for the maths",

she said. When a wave function disappears,
something new appears in its place. Where
exactly, when you aren't looking at it, is a

subatomic particle? Every time we make a
dive we see something new. This movie is
about the harm that repression can do yet

the film is just as repressive and sanitised
as the repression it aims to satirise. "Although
we take water samples at regular intervals, in

layman's terms we still know next to nothing
about the deep ocean", she said. Yes, but do
you prefer *Jason and the Argonauts* to *Clash*

of the Titans? "I don't care what the song is
about", she said, "*Golden Brown* is a glorious
piece of music and the best track The Stranglers

ever cut". At this point in the day it's all about
going for a walk in the hills. "Blue becomes black
as the darkness draws in upon us", she said.

All The Unknowns

There's nothing quite like the human
brain. Picking up on sarcasm can be
hard even for people but switching

to renewable water is a formidable task
and like it or not this decision sends a
disastrous signal. "It's only castles burning",

he sang. You can see the bees going
crazy over the east-facing flowers and
in the not-too-distant future we may

have to abandon the cities. "Then there's
the issue of what happens when people can't
pay", she said. Did you know that all the

water in the world has been here since the
dinosaurs? "I've studied the timing and the
inflection", she said. "I think I can pull it off".

Zero visibility requires an acute sense of
smell yet there's a lot of politicking going
on with regard to these pipelines. Are we

talking about a 'big bounce' rather than a
'big bang?' "This fish is a lurker", he said,
"though these mullet demand ultra-light tactics

and we may be in for a long wait". One day
we'll all pass away. "My tattoos let people
know how different I am", he said.

A New Construction

It's usually a matter of combining the
soft and the loud – contrast is every-
thing. "It's all about flavour not finesse",

she said. There is fierce competition
for limited resources and we may still
need to define our terms of negotiation.

Do you prefer your garlic strong and
hot or sweet and mellow? "It gives
me a bad taste in the mouth", she said.

"Survival will depend on how warm
these waters become but we may be
stepping into the unknown", she said.

Towards the end of the day the far west
could see an isolated heavy shower. "They
said they needed to change their clothes",

she said. When a wave function disappears
something new takes its place. Here we are
on the edge of the known, in contact with

the beauty of the unknown. Yet the work-
force of all developed countries is now
heavily service-oriented and it may soon

be a question of plugging yourself in rather
than taking more drugs. "Inside the sewer
we are measuring the echoes", she said.

A Likely Direction Of Travel

What stands in the way is the
market but we're talking hacking
here, not an inside leak. "I am the

winged avenger", he said. Isn't it
about time we built another fence?
This is the spot where Orson Welles

said the aliens had landed yet we
never get to live in someone else's
head and by the way are we thinking

in language or in images? "He was
on another planet most of the time",
she said, "and it sounds like a nice

planet to have been on". Yes, but with
so many debatable facts, perception often
creates the reality. "I want the writing to

be done by every member of the audience",
she said. This is no place for an outsider
and what we hear may not always be the

truth. Are you afraid of snakes? Yet the
nicest thing about the aperitif is that it
doesn't follow any rules and it's not just

cockroaches and crickets we're sharing our
cave with. "These surfaces are a little ruffled
while these have more activity", she said.

Divert, Deflect, Deceive And Deny

At the bottom of our grief is a terrible
anger. "It's a bit like being sent to
Coventry if you can't communicate",

he said. Perhaps she wasn't entirely
surprised when the balloon went up
but he felt he was living on the edge

and in any case these patterns are
always going to form. "I've always
enjoyed 'the grimace' yet we've all

got our personal 'found object' and
it's a matter of pyrotechnic swoops
and squiggles". The painting bled like

a wound. For the first time the origin
of a thought has been pinned down.
Soon our tree canopy will close over

and the light will be turned off. What
will they see in my wandering mind?
It can take a while to get used to new

wings and many never do yet the real
issue here may be about a split between
generations. "It's how you're saying it

that's more important than what you're
saying", he said. As she grows more conf-
ident a personal voice begins to emerge.

A New Pattern

Our titanic struggle is entering a new
phase. We have to keep things like
this under wraps but by all accounts
they don't half go some as well.
"It's just a slight tic in his flight/fight
response", she said. Yet our days are
getting shorter and there's a distinct
chill in the air. Meanwhile, back at the
house Steed and Mrs Peel are dancing.
If we start to move we will keep moving
and this is an example of the conservation
of energy. Why are so many people
disappearing into the wood? Here, the
relationship between artist and artefact
is crucial, while reptiles have scaly skins
and amphibians soft, moist ones.

As expected, the two countries signed an
agreement yesterday. Yet the continuous
babble of opinion is delightful as is the
odd juxtaposition of modernity and
antiquity. Birds are flocking at the
coastline and there's a surge of life
at sea. As his days pass the defender
finds that he's too busy to feed.
His work is innately elusive, just
as much as he's a master of discovery.
Yet our digital details are as imbued
with memories and emotions as the
physical possessions we leave behind.

An Indistinct Question

What is space? There's a
long night ahead. This one's
got a turned-up nose yet
we can always pay a visit
to every tattoo parlour in
the city. We're talking about
the return of the prodigal
here. Life is wild, wet and
full of surprises.

We're confident that the
maths will check out. It's a
deep, swirling pool and we
won't have long to wait.
"I love pattern", she said.
At this point we began
tunnelling beneath the
streets. Civilisation as
we know it is over.

We're here to guide you
through the process. Half
the catch is still in the sea
yet the plot makes as much
sense as the dialogue. Are
you in the swim? See if you
can scoop him up into the net.
Is it something or nothing?
a presence or an absence?

An Overpayment

"She's got a head full of
wasps", he said. Yet it
was more of an animated
debate than a riot and the
mechanisms of regulation
are intricate. It was just another
flurry of activity but the
anchovy is an anchor fish
that supports the whole ecosystem.

We could be fishing in the
canal or in either of the two
lakes today. Memory may
be located in the body as much
as in the mind. There are no
proper roads and no existing
maps. Life is more interesting
if there is cultural diversity.
How do we define illiteracy?

Are we about to enjoy ninety
per cent more volume? It is
not even a question of binary
opposition. Maps and swarms
are on the agenda today.
Theoretical biology suggests
that the presence of dyslexics
has survival value for humans.
In every case the aim is the same.

Flash Mob Flamenco

Arriving for lunch early I felt decidedly
out of place. With currencies wobbling
and shares uncertain, art continues to buck
the economic headwinds. No wonder rich
people are all so thin. Some of the locals
provide a cleaning service yet these bright
lights are all produced by the firefly squid.
If you know what to look for it's easy to
spot an atmospheric river. Next to arrive
is a sleeper shark.

If history is an evaluation of the past
surely it can's be taught without reference
to values. No matter how diverse the styles
these illustrations speak to us of an emerging
market. Her voice explorations of tv theme
tunes are remarkable and her *Dr Who* is
particularly haunting. Yet our default position
in everyday life is to use our intuition. As a result
her condition is easily overlooked. "At my age
it makes more sense to take the money".

Eating, for humans, has to do with
a whole social context. Yet the first
thing you notice is the quality of the light.
The more intelligent someone is the more
disastrous the results of their stupidity.
When ingested, the chemicals disrupt
key insect behaviours like navigation.
Precisely when did this transaction occur?
Finally, all these signals come together
in your brain. Large-scale stupidity is
even more damaging.

An Odd Phrase To Use

Should loss be stigmatised as illness?
It's impossible to say that someone
will or won't go on to develop one of these
conditions. Spring is a contested season.

"I believed that THEN & I believe
it now", he said. Yet his lip-synching
lagged slightly behind the music.
Don't these conditions run in the family?

So far attacks have only occurred
along the coasts. Shocking was what
he wanted to be & shocking was what
he was. "It's all a bit androgynous", she said.

Let's just say I have a picture in my head
of what happens in the final scene.
This time we had stronger legs & smaller
backpacks. What happens after the check?

Richard Thompson's in the background
discussing traditional ballads & playing
1952 Vincent Black Lightning – glorious.
It's a redefinition of self.

Here the path is more frequently interrupted
by fishing harbours. Is it *Beesley Street* or
Baker Street that Noel's talking about?
This is an answering machine – please go away!

I could do that for you if you can tell me
his name. "It's a pacu – a pink pacu". he said.
Do we have an organic connection to spring?
"We were ripe for exploitation and there was Bowie".

"If it's musical enough then you don't
need meaning", said Ian, while discussing
Beefheart & talking about decals. Now he
decides to allow himself to do what he does best.

Still Waters

Why do we love acoustic fuzz so much?
Another keyword might be 'intimacy' but
if you crunch numbers for long enough
you'll find patterns in almost anything.
To do this you will need a baiting needle.
There's a noticeable aversion to the word
'straightforward' tonight yet we are also
interested in the psychology of language
rather than its 'content'. Whatever else you
do tomorrow, please don't disturb the water.

"If you stop to think how you're doing it,
you won't be able to do it", she said. As
we opened the gate and entered the field
it was hovering directly overhead. How
are photons produced? For a charismatic
leader vagueness is valuable but it was
the disorientation of the dark which caused
us to shiver. These fish may be identified by
their scales. To make the maize more attractive
it can be soaked in an artificial sweetener.

More Indistinct Chatter

It's a tricky decision, whether to go
modern or stick with tradition but I'm
your doctor and you'll do exactly as I
tell you. Our addiction to oil comes at
a high price but do we really believe
we are the chosen people? "No more
emotional entanglements", she said.
Based on this information we'll decide
what to fish for and where to go. Are
you taking refuge in the weather again?
Other more agile visitors are attracted by
a potential feast yet these results may prove
catastrophic and it's not entirely clear what
is going on. A tumour continues to grow.

Jimi Hendrix At Gunnislake

Even the nosey bloke on the corner said
it might make things easier but the three-
line whips are the ones that really count
and now is the time to hoist our tree trunk
into position. Are frigate birds the pirates
of the high seas? Out here, feeding oppor-
tunities are always few and far between,
though we've been looking for the *Rising
Sun* for the past half hour or more and these
street signs are confusing beyond belief.
"I chose the Cadillac rather than the garrett",
said Wilko, but we're all thinking about
Jimi now as the weather is getting wilder and
darker. "It can happen any time", she said.

Another Good Cause

Is your gasp authentic or manufactured?
Yet the owls are not what they seem even
though you may be watching your weight
like a hawk. Some bricks are more important
than others – cornerstones, for example.
"Conditions here can change very fast", she
said, "but there are more things to life than
breaking and entering". Temperature is just
a measure of how fast things are moving around.
Disrespect the ice and you may go through.

Photons are all around us. Our ultimate
master of disguise is the octopus yet the
situation close to the coast is different.
Where do the colours in soap bubbles
come from? Tell us something about the
banana skin, starting now! Where the reefs
meet deeper waters, upturning currents bring
nutrients. This cloud turns data into excitement
but the corals close to shore are barely
hanging on. Our whale shark is a gentle giant.

Tide Tables

Look at the colour of the sun.
Look at the colour of that sun.
In winter the sea is much warmer
than the land. "See how the sun
shines brightly", she said. "This
is why the tiger needs the crab",
he said. "You can see from the
colour of my face that my body
is warm", she said. Yet it turns
out that airborne natural molecules
do indeed boost our health. "It's
just around the next bend again",
he said. Sphagnum, sphagnum,
moss, moss, moss, rotting feet,
trenchfoot.

Dealing With
The Damage

Offshore, one of nature's
great spectacles is about
to unfold.

How's this for synchronicity?

Just listening to *steptoe and
son* on radio 4 extra. They're
playing scrabble & albert is
winning because he's using
dirty words & harold can't
spell very well. As it finishes
I switch to the drama channel
for *the likely lads* where bob
& terry are talking about
scrabble & using dirty words

in order to win.

Learning To Adapt

Does the action always have
to be around transgression?

Yet we need to know where
we are going to go and this
includes arms, legs, luggage

and any electrical equipment
you may be using.

"Many of these pleasures
are unforbidden", he said.

At this point a second
highwayman approaches
the passengers.

Does the action always have
to be around transgression?

Waiting To Be Rescued

Up the stairs we go until we come to the tunnel.
Yet the possibilities of this situation spiralling
out of control are unreal. What's your involvement here?
Suddenly there's a moment when everything just clicks.

Do you have friends from before you were famous?
We are heading for a world in which we will live our
entire digital life in the cloud. Yet in the end I was
just using them to get through the day.

"We're certainly not under canvas any more", she said.
Yes, but what exactly does this invisible man look like?
Slow chords, elegant & restless & the physical power of
this lovely sway is overwhelming. A shrimp senses a threat.

At first the skeleton seems perfectly abandoned.
There's a tiger coming down the street & he has an
extraordinary ability to take you into oceans of desolation.
Smell is strongly tied to emotional memory.

This is like no other place on earth. When we get to the house
its door is wide open. How much of the subconscious gets
into your music? Yet it's an extremely dangerous place
for the unwary & there's a red sun on the horizon.

Their pace has quickened – they must have caught our scent.
When volcanoes erupt the ash flung out is electrically charged.
Yet this digital information has no physical existence we
can point to. A new pattern is beginning to emerge.

What exactly is it about relics? "It's not just Marc Bolan who
commands this sort of interest, you know". Different people
have different reactions to the same taste. Now the sardines
have no escape. Come into my mouth little fish.

We're stuck here until Sherlock Holmes comes along
& tells us what's going on. Do you find yourself avoiding
certain thoughts? This may create a scent trail hundreds of
yards long. Clouds spread across the sky like black ink.

A Wet Shave

There's a thunderstorm moving
in from the south. You can see
why it's called a triple tail and
we may have to chase him around
the boat. Yet we reserve the right
to edit items for clarity and style
though there's a gut reaction when
it comes to the shark. Have you
ever left anyone to pick up your tab?

"This isn't fat, you know, it's
relaxed muscle". Here we have
the grunting catfish. Even so, the
storm is bad enough and it may
be time to make an educated guess.
Yes, but do we treat the symptom
or its cause? "Keep back, there may
be another explosion", she said. Our
fish is now motionless in the margins.

Have you ever seen anything like
this before? Confusion on a ship
is something to fear yet it's a
different world down here and
we've created an atmosphere of
inertia. Such worries have already
spurred the formation of a 'slow
reading' movement. These ants know
exactly what they're dealing with.

Drinking To Excess

"I don't know if it's a catfish
or a carp", he said. Yes, but
what did I tell you about those
bollards? We're three minutes
ahead of schedule. Art is all
about creating new connections
between things yet the most
perfect example of swarm
intelligence lies with the insects.

Remember to keep mending
the line. Amazingly, these
creatures are staying at arms
length yet the geese are still
honking and all the particles
are flowing downstream.
What are the pros and cons
of annuities? This brings us to
the solar system's other oceans.

Retaliation is swift and
devastating. "Not a word of
this goes outside of this van –
do you understand?" It may
be a pirate show but you're
still top of the bill and there
are practicalities to resolve.
For the first time ever a space-
craft has landed on a comet.

A Controlled Explosion

"Never let a good crisis go to
waste", he said, yet noodling
is popular in Oklahoma, or so
we're told and underneath it all
there's a steely determination
which will become apparent.
With every step the air is getting
thinner. "This is the first time I've
had to saddle-up an elephant", she said.

It's so hot and humid we can
only work in short shifts.
"You'd better take over the
oars", she said. Yet on the
forest floor the remote cameras
are doing their job and what this
piece needs is some layered
harmonies. Everything points to
a gas attack but we have to investigate.

Rumours of tigers abound
but where are the tigers?
Details are emerging of the
victims and many questions
remain. Meanwhile, back
inside, a wobbly floorboard
leads the team to a secret
hiding place. Demonstrations
have all been banned.

It's a soft target with minimal
security and stocks of blood
are running low. These strange
looking objects are often taken
for UFO's but intelligence is

crucial and the next twenty four hours will be critical. We may never be able to go there but we can have some idea of what the journey could be like.

A Sea Of Tranquillity

From the inside they are
a thing of great beauty
yet surfing burns a lot
of energy and our eerie
silence is only broken
in the spring. Are you
losing weight and feeling
great? There is blood
everywhere, dead bodies
everywhere. These leaves
should not be shed. Are
you making a date with
drama? The figure of death
comes at the end of every
scene and carries someone off.

A Judicial Enquiry

At the moment the world is
awash with oil but you're

not you when you're hungry
and it would seem that some-
one is on our trail.

Are you getting a good grip?

A swirling
pattern
in the water
reveals its presence.

Feedback and distortion
are used to dazzling effect.

Nothing was warm about
him except his smile.

Then They Stopped Clapping

Normal breathing is quiet & easy.
Let us pause for a moment
to review the patient's situation.
Why should the bees just pack up and leave?

Yet it was a blow in the face
to conventional thinking &
these pools are teeming with life.
If possible, abandon your car before it sinks.

& then there was the group's
visual image, which was extreme,
even for the time. Who is this man
& what is he doing in my house?

I'm always interested in people
with a criminal record yet they learn
to do this spontaneously by holding
their breath & pulling in their abdomens.

We were soon joined by
a solitary dancer & people clapping.
This show opens with a walk
through the streets of a city.

"I was out with my family one day
when I was dragged into a car by a fan",
she said. Once inside, we instantly
move at a slower pace.

Sandy shores tend to be gentle & sloping.
From a distance they look purely decorative
but as you get closer you can see the details.
This complex glass structure is a marvel of modern design.

As we push deeper we hope the beasts
will start to show themselves. "What do
you mean by 'signs of possession'", she asked.
Of course, you won't get him to corroborate any of this.

A Series Of Photographs

Once again, nothing is what it seems.
Purists may be uneasy about these
developments yet your scruples seem
very provincial and our results are
always unusual. Clearly not every
clamouring crowd is violent but leaving
everything to nature is risky and it's
the only document we have to back-up
our claim. "I'm not a fan of bait-boats
but they can be really effective", he said.

Taste is paramount. "Yes, but can you
detect nutmeg and mace", she asked.
Once again, we have the theme of a rebel
who never surrenders. Is this a random
pattern or an interference pattern? Yet the
files that do exist leave a trail of evidence.
Are we going in armed? In six weeks or
so we will all face freezing temperatures
and these leafy invaders are hard to control.
If you were a barbel where would you live?

A Following

A fox is not a wanton killer but an intelligent opportunist
who thinks ahead. Yet bridges may be created horizontally
and vertically, with no more than two bridges between any
pair of islands. We too are part of an elaborate game of pick
'n' mix and the best of today's sunshine will be in the east.
Thick bands of textured colour, ranging from lemon yellow
to burgundy red, cover the canvas. Is commercial fishing
sustainable? Let's find someone who can give us the facts.
At this point he closed the front door behind him and hung
up his dripping raincoat.

"Here we have a trumpet, nudity and the perfect way to
answer the question have you put on weight?", she said.
Yet no number can appear more than once in a dotted area
and this is one survival strategy we can all share. Have you
ever been in Glasgow on a Saturday night? If there are lots
of salmon around the grizzlies will eat only brains and caviar.
Yet consumers pay more attention to the label than the shape
and there's always the temptation to specialise. Climate is what
you expect while weather is what you get. These days, in opera,
the soprano is often the heroine and usually gets her man.

A Cult Status

Sometimes ideas arrive in the form of a dream.
Whatever happened to the log lady? Meanwhile,
the production of fish-food sticks is on the way.
Is this simply a thought experiment? This one
is large and orange and juicy and it's like a giant
everlasting gobstopper. "I'm just going to flick a
float out", he said. Available in black, purple or
chic brown, these beauties can be embossed or
engraved. Yes but is this a dream or a nightmare?
Punishment may include dismissal or formal reprimand.

Perhaps you prefer the vintage-looking floral
design with a mint green background? We may
also need an independent body to separate fact
from fiction. Yes but what about the dodgy dossier?
"You can always try the magic bones", she said.
What kind of thing could have done that? Yet our
records show that the above property has become
unoccupied. Today we're using high-visibility pop-
ups. What are the basic properties of photons?
At the end of the day a cage is just a cage.

Let The Fish Breathe

What we're getting now is a lot of white noise.
Yes, but have you signed anything yet? When
I first saw him I thought he'd been hit by a car.
What sort of long-term impact is this going to have?

"You're a sailor. Did you never hear of the plague?"
Suddenly, you're a man with no identity, in a police
state where everyone is closely monitored. He's part
of the remnant stock, long before the trout were here.

This is a species that saw the dinosaurs come & go.
What of the contemporary crusade to 'liberate' world
markets? It's a bold evolution of shock therapy yet also
a question of perception. The word torture is never used.

How come I'm the big cheese around here? Yet he
was just an ordinary bloke who made his living as
a fisherman. Recent surveys have found there are
ten species of fish in this lake. What exactly is a bubble?

He really is the river wolf. Do you have any more
thoughts about the garden? The only thing that stops
a composer thinking about music is rigor mortis yet
you can't seriously say that rockpools lack drama.

There is no imminent threat to the public or property.
"This is the first time I've ever watched a spider weave
an entire web, though I've seen it before in a dream."
I expect you want to cut it out & put it in your scrapbook.

Her impact on women's lives will continue to be debated
as a promise of spring lingers in every complex mouthful.
We have no contingency plan but how about animals that
live in the water? This whole area is alive with pike.

All the creatures in the rockpool must be constantly alert yet pull as I might the rabbit refused to come out of its hat. As a form of intellectual imperialism it was certainly unabashed. Who *do* we trust to regulate the regulators?

Reading The Water

Once again we're
looking at a soft
target. "You don't
go skinny-dipping
with snapping turtles",
he said. Yet it could
be that plagiarism
is a key intellectual
device and young,
rigorous shoots are
what we want. Should
we welcome the era
of driverless cars?
Here's the dent, made
by the heel as it hits
the ground running.
How real are the tensions
at the top of the party?
"No, it's not a different
thing entirely", he said.
For those in thrall to its
ideas representation is
dead yet this swim has
all the hallmarks of a
hotspot. "It's a projection,
not a fact", he said, "and
our aim is always to build
legitimacy". It's a big,
open expanse of water
and there are few trees.
Today there will be
fireworks.

A Vehicle Approaches

Whoever it is
they are living
on borrowed
time. Are we
talking process
or product here?
Delicate fabrics
may be another
matter but some-
times an iceberg
will flip right
over in front of
your eyes. In this
instance it's not
so clear cut though
for some reason
you haven't taken
this into consideration.
Of course, the secret
of parsley soup
lies in the parsley
yet this issue is one
of consumption,
not production.
"That old moon
river", she said,
"it's wider than
a mile". Do you
see a connection
between loneliness
and inner voices?
A message in a
bottle which has
washed up more

than 100 years
after it was thrown
in the sea has been
confirmed as the
world's oldest.

A Chink In Our Armour

Are things about to
come tumbling down?
With the wind at their
backs the pirates charged.
"Europe needs to think
again", he said. It's all
about scratching a living
from things that others
throw away. Our antidote
to a lie may indeed be a
fiction but the driving
force of imperialism is
always the economy.
Are we looking at a new
magic bullet? What's your
take on what's going on
at the moment? It's a chub,
a chub on a plug. Yet once
again we're talking about
characters on the edge.
"Empires rise and empires
fall", she said. Bizarre
creatures appear as if from
nowhere yet the lower your
body temperature the slower
you age. "These are the cats
that break all the rules",
she said. Yet something
is going wrong with our
powers of navigation and
the consequences are deadly.
Isn't empire the default
position of human history?

Adapting To
The Situation

Are ideas important
in art? What's being
talked about here is
gender-equality yet there
is no chance of an
immediate coup and
we're in for a severe
pruning. Here we have
a massive squandering
of talent. "Yes, but it's
the reputation of these
images which creates
a sense of boredom",
he said. What is it that
you want me to do?
"Such wonky variation",
she said. Yet we scoured
the streets for junk and
for the throwaway textures
of the city. Who knows
what may lurk beneath
the turbulent current?
Your hours may not be
specified but payment
will be made on submission
of a monthly pay claim.
Are you a wild-eyed loon
standing at the gates of
oblivion? "First of all,
it's wrong to blame the
zander", he said. Are you
suppressing your painterly
touch? Meanwhile, some-
thing big has grabbed hold

at last and it's time to start
talking in riddles again.

Into The Blue

"I've seen tomorrow
and it's terrifying",
he said. We wade
ashore, weary, after
an hour of deep-water
swimming. Anything
with body heat stands
out. To unlock these
secrets we decide to
film at night yet our
dependence on satellites
is terrifying. A pandemic
threat may not be new
but it remains very real.
Beneath the surface
a network of currents
is constantly on the
move. Any quick
thoughts? "We need
better sharing of
information", she said.
What's fantastic about
this place is that it's
right on everyone's
doorsteps. Are you
lost in the flow?
Each hunter sends
out a series of clicks
then listens for returning
echoes. Our sky looks
milky this afternoon
and there are isolated
patches of richness.
"We are storytellers",
she said. When the frigate

bird joins the hunt, our
flying fish is caught
between the devil and
the deep blue sea.

Black Boots

It's all a matter of entering a café and looking
for your friend. "Today we're using a mixture
of casters and hempseed", she said. Yet the light

is still leaking into the street and these are artists
who have been lost to history. You're the guy in
the audience and I'm the guy on the flying trapeze.

"This is the first time that the entire city has been
mapped", she said. Let's just take this hook out
before we're bitten. It may be time to give our

Chinese rocket a final tweak. You should keep the
bale arm open as there are bandits at ten o'clock.
There may be a pattern here but we have yet to

find it and by the way another fudge is not an
option. "It's woven into our vernacular", he said,
"but anything worth doing is worth doing quickly".

There's obviously something dodgy going on here
and an acceleration of information flow may also
have an effect on cognition. Yes, but has punctuation

come to a standstill and why is it called an ampersand?
Our chef is on the fiddle. As a result we've set out to
conduct a systematic search of all the scientific literature.

Once ashore we soon warm up. Do you feel the
issues have been spelt out and the ground well-
prepared? It's time to sweat the vegetables.

Covering The Water

After a morning's fishing our nets remain empty.
"It's the direction of travel", she said. At least it
shows that the method is still working and all

priority will be given to those in busy areas.
Basic spoons and spinners are on the agenda
today as dead-baiting has proved unproductive.

It's all a matter of leaving the light to speak through
the paint. Is social mobility still a source of great
anxiety? When the next species is tagged, striking

differences are recorded yet it may be a question of
particles rather than waves. Does a chalk landscape
produce chalk artists and chalk writers? "This is the

standard of cooperation we need to achieve", she said.
As our survey expands we should get a clearer picture
but the lights remain on and the title track was conceived

closer to home. Do these boundaries hold us in or
hold us back? When it comes to your eyes, don't
compromise. Yes, but she's always going up and

down the escalator and this is about victimising
extremely vulnerable people. "This looks the way
I need it to sound", she said. It's a light-tackle outfit

and everything has to be just right. "It's a three-bearded
rockling", she said. Other colour signals have a different
meaning. Like the milky way, andromeda is a spiral galaxy.

Sometimes It Just Happens

It's always a bare-knuckle fight if you like
though advertising may well rely on false-
memory syndrome. Hence the hollow centre.

If you're over the limit you're over the limit.
Voting twice is a crime but this is to do with
removing names from the voting rolls. Are we

talking about another rigged economy here?
Otherwise, notions of justice are submerged
under a new vengefulness. It's all a matter of

intercepting the incoming sunlight and this is
the habitat of our dreams, dreamed by us and
created by us. Your calculations should be

performed from left to right yet the fish in this lake
are shared out only once a year. It's an impressive
fish, the goliath grouper, but we are talking here

about things which are extremely tiny. Next, we
glue plastic flanges onto each end of the bellows
where the image becomes crude and vicious.

Perhaps these fish only bite in self-defence when they
are disturbed. When you read a novel do you hear the
voices in your head? It's crisp, light and full of fruit.

With war, the satire map takes on a brutal tone
yet a complex and more beautiful structure emerges.
Here we can see how the neutrons are assembled.

The Sunlit Uplands

A change of personnel may bring
a change in fortune and there's no
sign of the herring being pushed

to the surface. When we are faced
with the void we fill up the space
with stuff yet the status quo is not

an option and one way or another
civil society will fight back. Yes,
but is it possible to avoid projection?

It was an illegal purge of the voting
rolls and our fiscal policy needs to
be recast. Look at the tail on that.

Deep or shallow? It's all up to the
viewer. Here we have a patchwork
pieced together from a multitude of

fabrics yet progress has been snail-
slow and extremely risky. Today, it's
all about stealth and concealment but

if you go into a swim with a slower
flow you can always reduce your
shotting. First we have to eliminate

family members from our enquiries. It's
another offshore hotspot yet everything
is tending towards disorder all the time.

Hide And Seek

"I really believed that tens of thousands of people
would die unless I did what the voices said", she said.
Are you an outsider or an amateur? Yes, but did you

know a quarter of your bones are in your feet? "Once
again the universe was interesting to me", she said,
"yet I chose you for what you were, not what you've

become". You should take the footpath opposite, going
diagonally right across the field. "For a dace, that's not
a bad fish at all", he said. Are we about to change our

essential argument? Yet we need to know where we are
going to go and there has to be an international settlement
at some point. "I'm feeling some residual anger", she said,

"and your newspaper is reporting a series of lies". Are we
playing ducks and drakes now? Even in the most famous
of Greek dishes, east meets west yet these dippers are

incredibly territorial and another Atlantic storm is brewing.
"There's a dreamy sadness in your eyes", he said. It's a funny
old world but these leadership polls are very interesting and

here we have an alpine chalet with palm trees outside.
"What if I was away for months," she asked. Anyone
for tennis? Unless you really know what you're doing

you probably don't want to find yourself at the top of a
mountain at night. "Please excuse my descent into the
demotic," she said. It's either boots on the ground or

nothing this time yet few in government even know the
agency exists. Are you a sharp-suited spy? "Adolescence
is the only time we learn anything", he said.

www.ingramcontent.com/pod-product-compliance
Lightning Source LLC
Chambersburg PA
CBHW022201080426
42734CB00006B/536